how to draw
fun characters

3dtotal KIDS

3dtotal KIDS

Email: publishing@3dtotal.com
Website: www.3dtotal.com

How to Draw Fun Characters © 2023, 3dtotal Publishing. All rights reserved. No part of this book can be reproduced in any form or by any means, without the prior written consent of the publisher.

First published in the United Kingdom, 2023, by 3dtotal Kids, an imprint of 3dtotal Publishing.

Address: 3dtotal.com Ltd, 29 Foregate Street, Worcester, WR1 1DS, United Kingdom.

Soft cover ISBN: 978-1-912843-74-9
Printed and bound in China
by C&C Offset Printing Co., Ltd

Written & illustrated by Erin Hunting

Editor: Marisa Lewis
Designer: Fiona Tarbet
Lead Editor: Samantha Rigby
Lead Designer: Joseph Cartwright
Studio Manager: Simon Morse
Managing Director: Tom Greenway

At 3dtotal Publishing we give 50% of our net profits to charities that help people, animals, and our planet. We also plant one tree for every book we sell.

Erin Hunting is a Melbourne-based illustrator and character designer who loves to create drawings for picture books and comics.
erinhunting.com

This book belongs to...

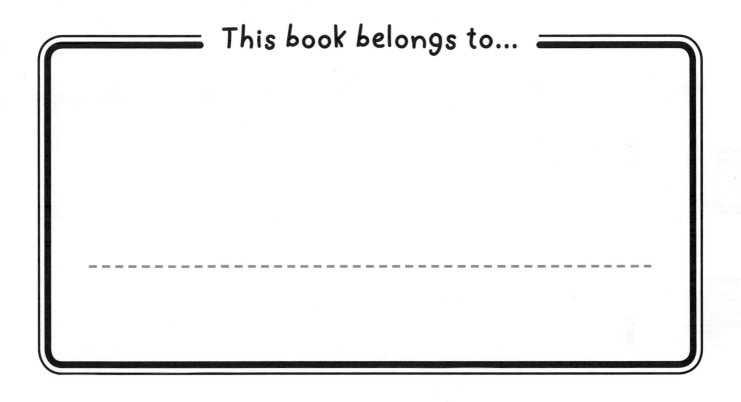

All you'll need is something to draw with:

crayons

pens

pencils

markers

Whatever you like!

And also paper!
It can be loose or in a sketchbook:

So come on, let's have some fun!

Start here

keep going

nearly there

All done!

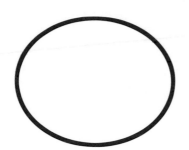
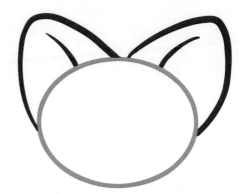

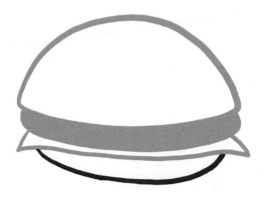

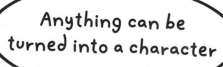

Anything can be turned into a character

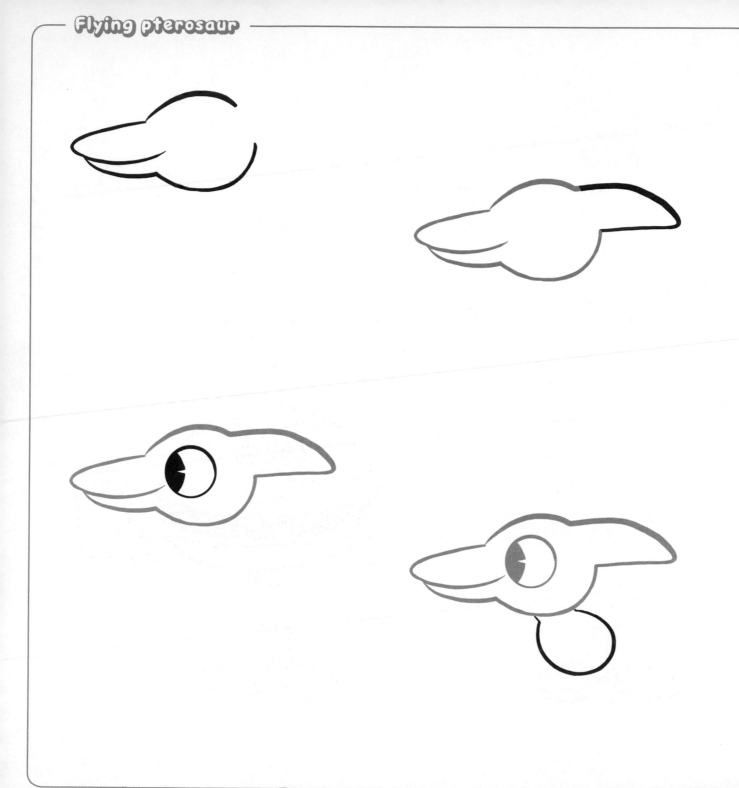

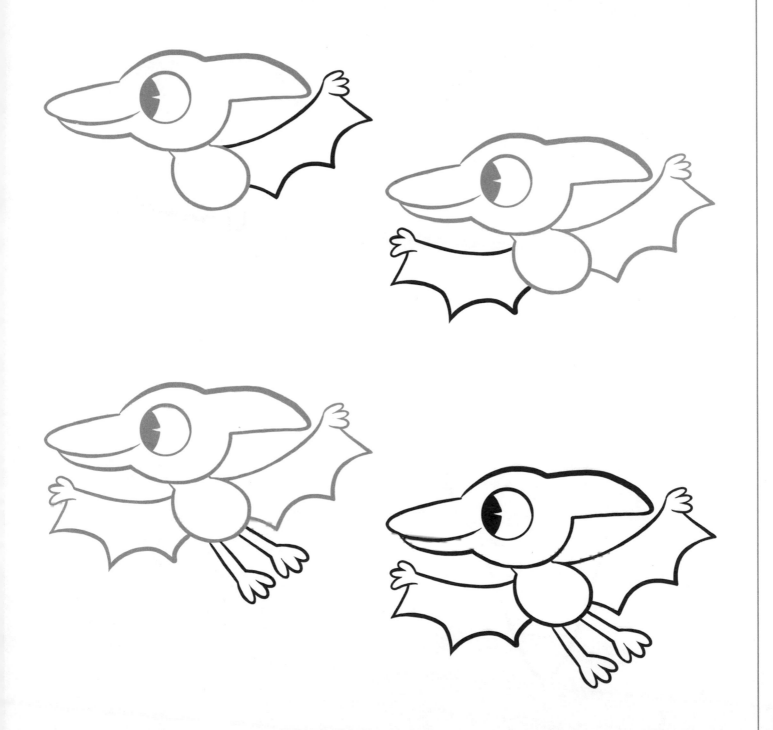

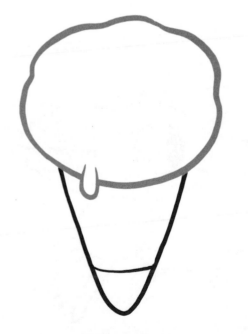

Different eyebrows can change someone's expression.

A little worried!

Calm and happy!

Can you think of other expressions to draw?

Fierce and frowny!

How about raising just one eyebrow?

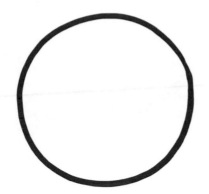
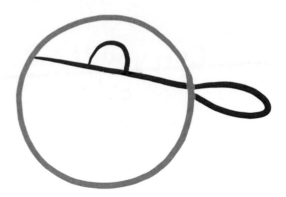

Alien in a spaceship

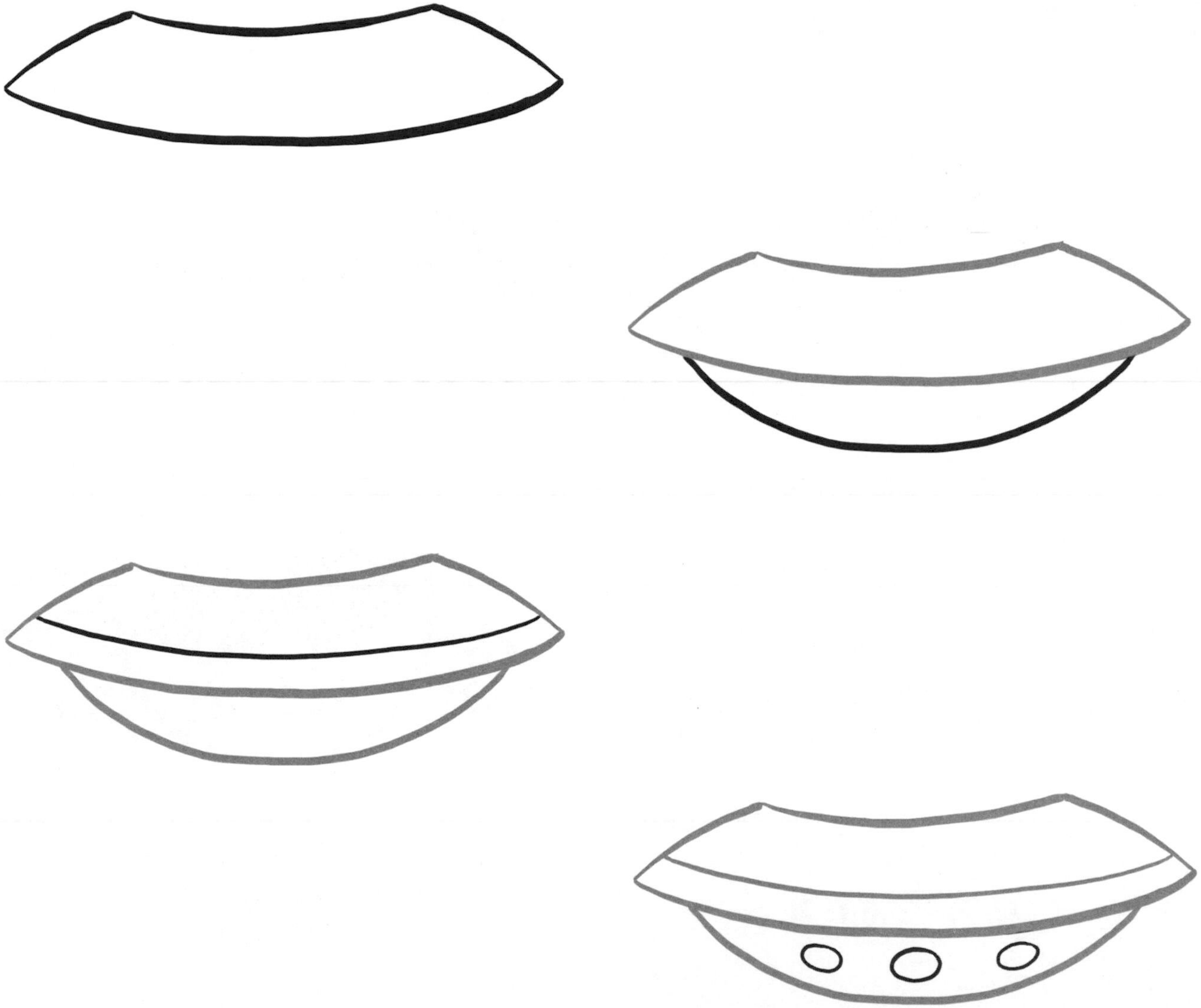

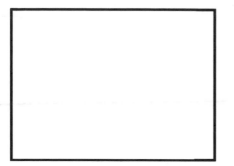

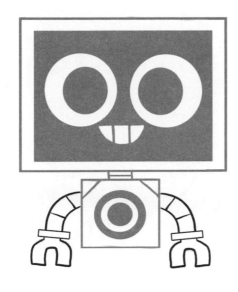

Gingerbread man

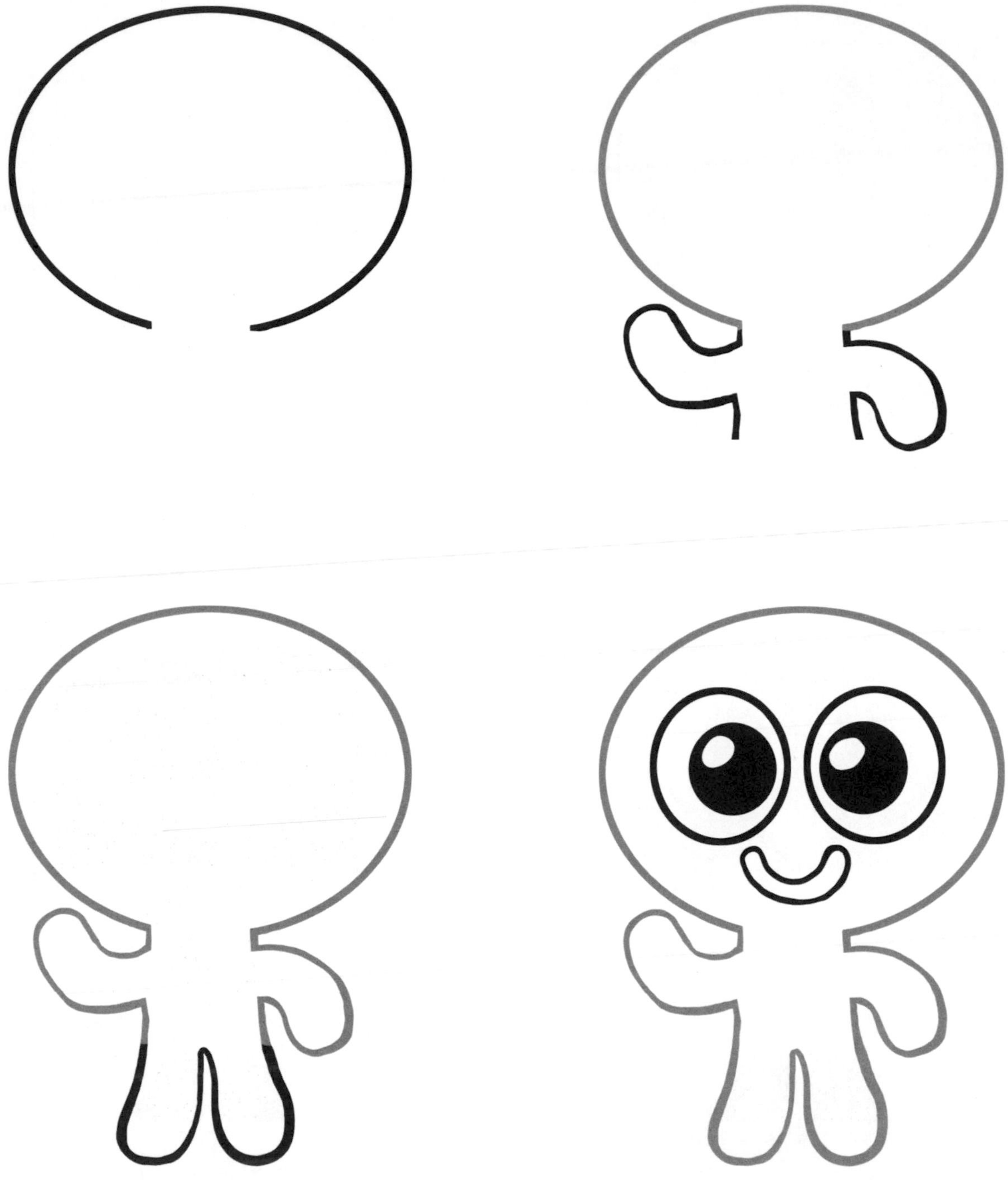

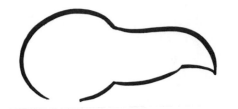

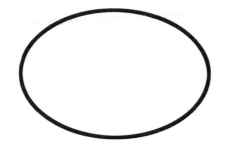

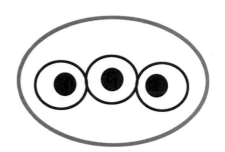

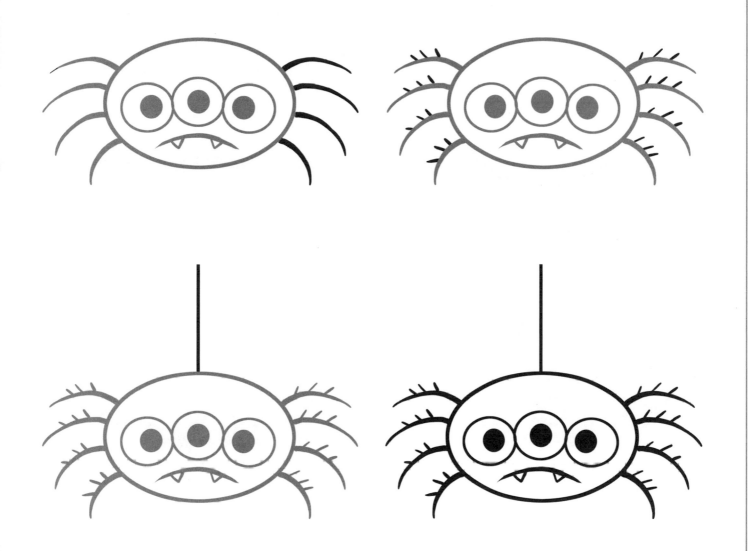

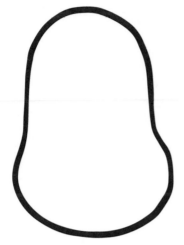

Can you draw your own monsters? Here are some to inspire you!

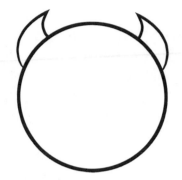

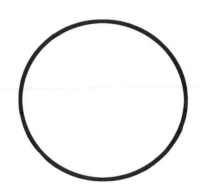

Spooky ghost

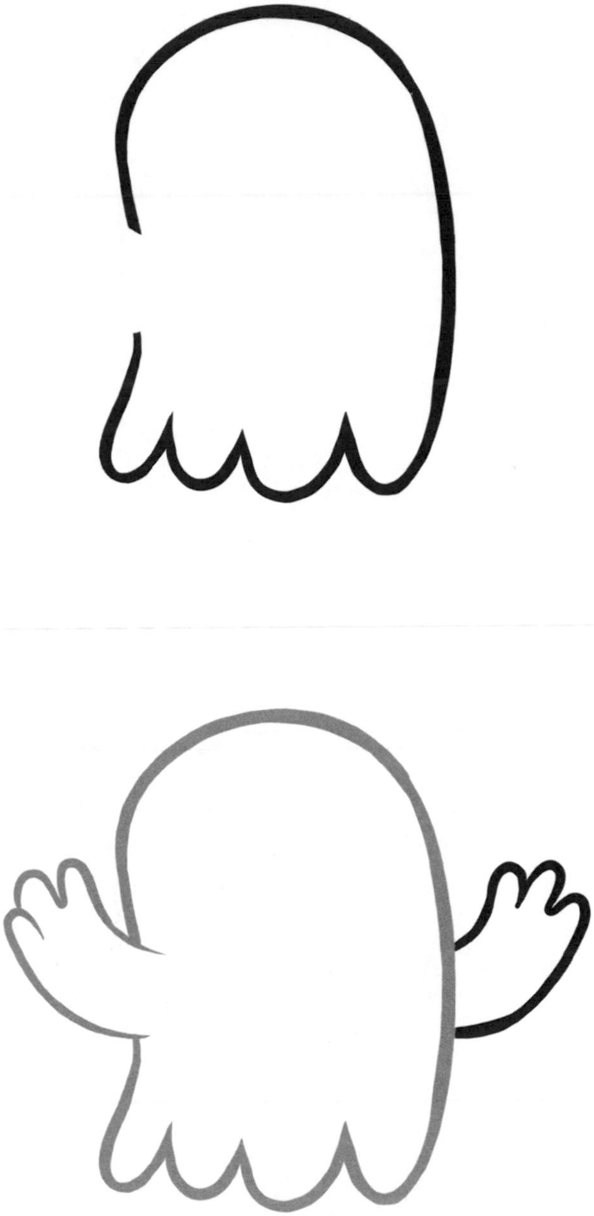

What hobbies can a monster have?

Placing the face in different areas of the head totally changes the character!

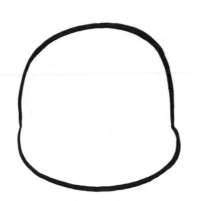

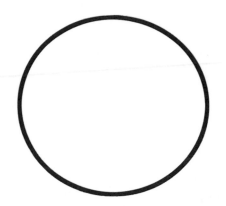

Different expressions are fun to draw.

Happy

Annoyed

Try drawing them on different things!

Confused

Tired

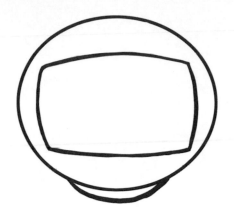

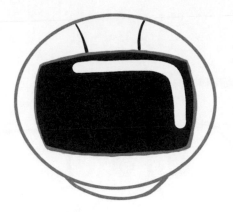

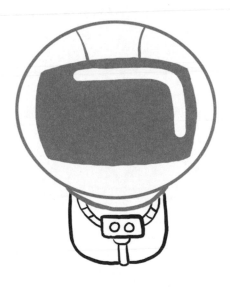

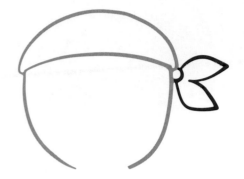

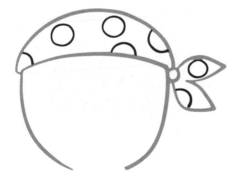

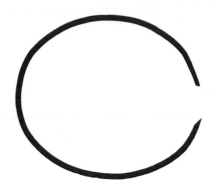

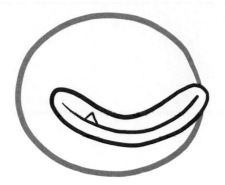

Cute cactus

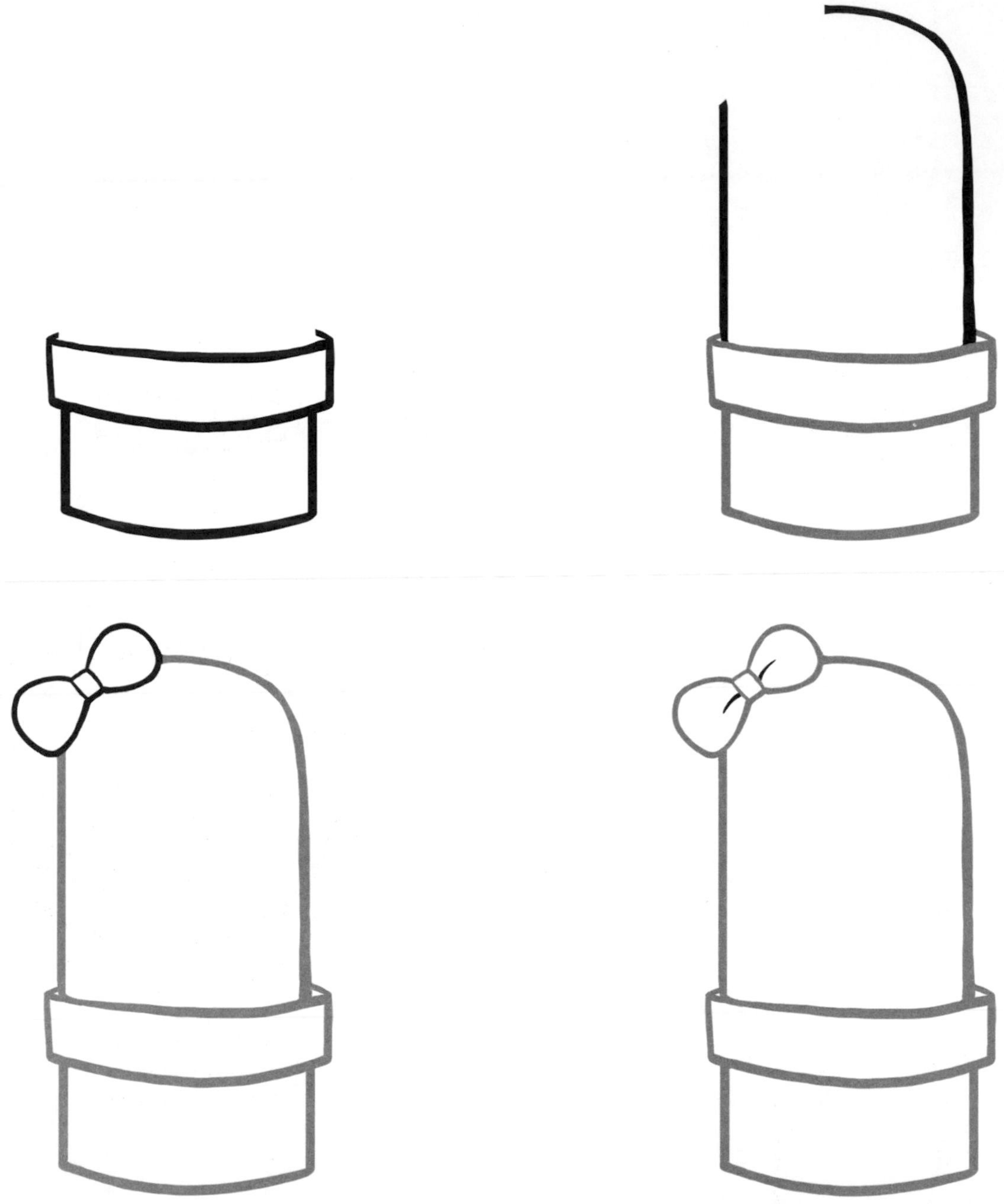

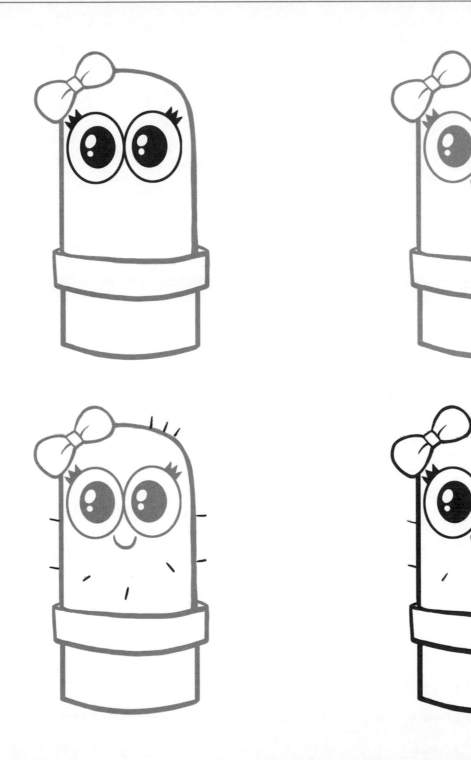

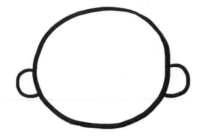

Worried

Silly

Try changing a character's expression
to show their mood!

Angry

Cute

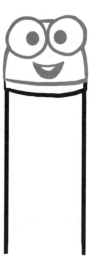

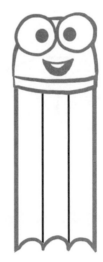
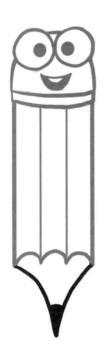

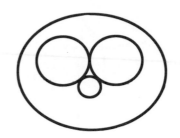

Now we're cooking!

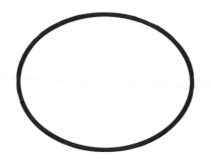

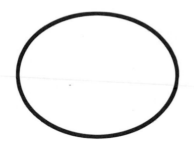

His eyebrows make him look mean!

You've finished this book!

You can go back and practise
drawing the characters again,
or make up your own.
Have fun drawing!